American Twelfth Night

AND OTHER POEMS

BY

SISTER M. MADELEVA, C.S.C.

THE MACMILLAN COMPANY · NEW YORK

1955

For

Saint Mary's College, Notre Dame

Our Indiana Centenary

Contents

American Twelfth Night

AND OTHER POEMS

David

Speak, young boy of God;
When blossoms the predilect flower of Jesse's quick rod?
Out of Saba when come those grave kings by a light
Newborn to the night?

The mountains of Juda, when leap they with laughter and mirth
At a Bethlehem birth?
Speak, David, child-seer of star and of sky;
The time, is it nigh?

A flower of Jesse, a shepherd you are,
A king and a star,
A song to the glory of God, and a singer who thrills
All the Judean hills.
These signs, are they met and embraced and come true,
Or frustrate in you?

Nay, the root and the rod and the bud have their use and their hour,
But Christ is the Flower.
A shepherd but not to be led to the slaughter am I,
To bleed and to die;

A king who the robe of a fool and the thorn crown has known
In vision alone;
A singer whose heart must cry out through the joy of his song,
"How long, Lord,—how long?"
A watcher who looks through the mist over Bethlehem's hills
        for a thousand slow years,—
A mist that is tears.

Dialogue

A Word, a Word
Thou, Lord, didst utter which Thy willing handmaid heard,
And infinite, small Life within my own life breathed and stirred.

A blessed space
My Lord in me and I in Him found resting place;
In such divine repose I waited, silent and full of grace.

Answer is nigh;
O God, I lift a Child up heart-and-heaven high
And say, "This is my Flesh and Blood;" Thy Word is my reply.

Swaddling Clothes

My days are all white with wonder, the wonder of stitching
    and sewing,
Making a spotless garment for Mary's spotless Son;
My hours are bright with joy as I watch the small robe growing,
The little robe of love that will compass the infinite One.

Love is the cloth it is made from; my heart possesses no other;
Love is the pattern, too, that I trace with unfaltering care;
Love is my double thread; the love of the Son and the mother;
Woven throughout of love, think you it will be fair?

Aye, and the mother Mary will let her little One wear it,—
He Who has never in aught save divinity been arrayed,—
All upon Christmas morning; O heart of me, can you bear it,
The joy of your God appareled in raiment your love has made!

Possession

I cannot chant the angels' hymn
As did the hosts of seraphim.

I cannot even cross the wild
As shepherds did, to find the Child.

I cannot shine, a living star,
To guide grave magi from afar.

I have no incense, myrrh, or gold
For gift as had the kings of old.

In all the world there is nowhere
A place so poor, a spot so bare

Save the rude cave at Bethlehem town
Where Christ, my Savior, laid Him down.

Because I am like that mean stall
I may possess Him most of all.

Ways

God has most simple ways.
He likes a stable's covering,
And little lambs that shepherds bring.
His majesty aside He lays,
You would not know He is a King,
He has such humble ways.

See, where He lies, quite sweet and small,
A Baby in an ox's stall
Smiling to meet His mother's gaze.
You could not fear this God at all,
He has such tender ways.

But look you, how the heavens blaze!
And hark you, what angelic praise
Resounds! Indeed, He is a King,
And these be Godlike ways.

Joseph

I am with various griefs acquainted well;
Through tense and tender days at Nazareth
I walked with anguish bitterer than death,
And doubt less merciful and kind than hell.
There, too, came utter loneliness to dwell,
(My loved one tarrying with Elizabeth).
I have not piteous word nor piteous breath
The bitterness of Bethlehem to tell.

It is not bitterness will break my heart,
But this: a mother's smile, a Babe's weak cry,
A little cheek to stroke, a hand to kiss!
Ah! I could push the stars of heaven apart,
And dare the awe-full face of God most high
For strength to bear the ecstasy of this!

Stars

We are the stars that have watched the night skies with the prophets
    of old;
We are the magi from out of the East; we are bringers of gold.

Heaven has incense of praise from censers seraphic to bring;
Earth, the world-weary, bears bitter-sweet treasure of myrrh to the
    King.

Homage of incense and myrrh for a God and a Saviour are meet;
We are your stars, little King, and we scatter the gold of ourselves at
    Your feet.

A Word for Shepherds and Angels

I spoke to Gabriel and was not afraid;
But to these herdsmen, hardy keepers of sheep,
And their singing midnight skies, what reply shall be made?

I may say to them—it were a gracious thing to do—
"My Son when grown to a man, my Child asleep,
He will care for flocks; He will be a shepherd, too."

Then mayhap their hearts will be opened as mine, with pain;
They may understand how my first-born, my only One
Will be our unblemished Lamb—and slain, and slain!

Angels and shepherds and I have known, have heard
Tidings to shatter the earth and amaze the sun.
Angels and shepherds, tonight I bring you the Word.

American Twelfth Night

Three men have just arrived,
Wise men from the West,
The continent of Christopher Columbus,
The Christ-bearer, the Dove.
They have journeyed far;
They have travelled a bitter way,
Seeking You to adore You.

The gifts they offer are past price, past precedent.

One brings You a lost continent.
One brings You his ambiguous liberty.
One brings his wealth of hallowed and unhallowed gold.

Red, black, and white, they come to You as brothers.

Make them, O Christ, three in one after Your image!
Keep them, O God, one in three in Your own likeness.

Christmas: Elizabeth Watches the Night Sky

I think the clouds tonight
Are lambs and wayward sheep
Huddled and lost and white.
My boy stirs in his sleep!

At midnight he awoke
As at an uttered word.
I only guess who spoke
And what he heard.

His eyes, before he slept,
Grew deep as prophets' are.
Up from their darkness leapt
Light like a star.

Two clouds drift in the blue.
How strangely moved I am!
They are like a lone ewe
And her young lamb.

A Song of Bedlam Inn

My gate stands open,
My window alight;
I shall wait at the threshold
Through the still night.

And if my love comes
On tired feet,
I shall hear his footsteps
In the still street.

I shall lift the latch
Like a broken wing,
For he knows my life
Is a shattered thing.

I shall open the door
With a broken cry,
For the night that I let
My love pass by.

But I shall say
No word at all.
For the sound of his step,
For his low call

My gate stands open,
My window alight.
My love and your love
Will come tonight.

Christmas in Provence

I

MIDNIGHT MASS

Tonight this city seated on a hill
Wears its mediaeval fortress like a crown
Above a brow too peace-possessed to frown.
Its ancient church watches the darkness fill
With quiet aureoles of light that spill
Through little streets that clamber up the town.
Here ancient, royal kings have laid them down,
And here, this night, a King will rest Him still.

I had not known that night could be so holy;
I had not thought that peace could be so deep.
O passion of night and peace, possess me solely!
O passion of love, be mine this night to keep!
O little climbing streets, lead me up slowly
To where the King I wait for lies asleep!

II

THE SERENADE

This age-old church, dream-stricken yesterday,
Has wakened into loveliness and light
And all Provence is in its arms tonight,
And all its tambourines and fifes are gay.
The dull, encumbering ages fall away;
Templar and king kneel in the ancient rite
With torches' blaze and candles tall and white
And a Child cradled on the fresh-strewn hay.

Then the night fills with song, laughing and leaping,
This music of a thousand lyric years,
A serenade of love where love lies sleeping,
The minstrelsy of God where God appears,
And where I kneel, bemused, song-shaken, weeping,
A happy-hearted troubadour in tears.

Christmas Eve

I journeyed down to Bethlehem
In deep peace on a winter day.
I think a young girl and a man
Were with me on the way.

And in the little town at dusk
The young girl waited in the street.
The stones and I were very glad
With kissing of her feet.

A tender wind encompassed her;
The waiting world, the listening air,
The watching stars grew sweet and white
With kissing of her hair.

The earth was wise as any child
Because she was so young and wise,
And all the dark was luminous
With looking in her eyes.

Tonight I wait upon my knees
Beside her in this quiet place,
Loving the wonder in her heart,
The wonder in her face.

Bethlehem

On Christmas eve in Bethlehem town
The shadows fall; the night comes down;
The stars shine clear; the winds grow mild;
An inn stands open for a Child
On Christmas eve in Bethlehem town.

In Bethlehem on Christmas day
One manger is fresh strewn with hay,
And you will find a young Child there,
And you will find a lady fair
In Bethlehem on Christmas day.

All roads must lead to Bethlehem;
All men at last must follow them;
And be you great or be you small
The sweet Lord Jesus bless you all
Upon the roads to Bethlehem.

Christmas Night 1940

There is a night too circumspect for stars,
A night too still and suppliant for song.
Kings do not walk abroad nor shepherds watch.
None save a Child is strong.

This night has fallen; more desired than dawn
The splendor of a Child will wake the skies.
Peace will be in His heart and on His lips,
And pity in His eyes.

Voices are crying through the wilderness
And children wander in a nameless land.
This night a Child is born. Some know His name
And some may understand.

New Things and Old

Christmas 1941

The dark is shattered
With wild, new fear;
An ass's feet stumbling
Is the sound that I hear.

The night is brighter
Than day should be;
A strange star's splendor
Is the light that I see.

And above the terror
Of earth and sky
I can hear, if I listen,
A young Child's cry;

I can see, if I look,
Legions of wings,
And a woman who ponders
On all these things.

Sheepfolds

The shepherds are stricken; the sheep have fled;
Their folds are broken, their watch-fires dead.

Not only the lost and wayward one;
The ninety-nine, they, too, are undone.

The laden ewes, the driven sheep,
Where can they lay their young to sleep?

This Lamb, new-born and weak and cold,
This Lamb of God,—will you be His fold?

To Be Enrolled

This is the month for census-taking.
I come to be enrolled in Bethlehem,
The House of Bread, to which I legally belong.

Already I foresee that not one of its hostels will receive me.
I shall seek lodging in a manger-cave at the town's edge.
Joseph, my kinsman, will be there
With Mary, his espoused wife, and her Child
Who is the Son of God.

This year and every year He comes to Bethlehem
To be enrolled among the sons of men.
And I, who am the merest of them,
I also am a son of God.
I also come to be enrolled with **Him.**

Christmas

This is the hour to which all hours lead.
The table is spread with fine white linen.
Bread and wine and water are set out.
A great book stands ready from which the prayers and
    history of this day will be read.
We are to eat by candlelight.
The tapers are already burning.
This is a feast of love.
Christ is our host.
You and I are to be His guests.
This is Christ's Mass.
It is the hour to which all hours lead.

The Light

You do not know, you cannot, cannot guess
Across what burning sands I come to you;
Over what difficult seas, upon what new
Hard ways of exile, ways of loneliness.

You did not think of gifts—my piteous three;
Worthy I thought them—kings had such of old.
Do you keep but the frankincense and gold,
And leave the bitterness of myrrh to me.

Bid me, I will return into the night.
Remember only, you who merciful are,
I found you by the shining of a star,
So I must walk forever in its light.

Christmas Song

The earth is very beautiful with stars
And there are wise men yet who love their light,
Shepherds who watch their flocks and gather songs
From the still night.

And though the hostels of the world be thronged,
Its mangers wait, its stable doors swing wide.
Mary, young girl, this is their hour and yours;
Come, come inside!

Jesus, young child, content You here to lie
Among clean kine and men bemused with awe.
Remember, dearling, when You made Your world
You willed this straw.

The world is blind; the world is Bethlehem
But over it Your stars are very bright.
With weak and wise, with Mary here I am,
Young child, tonight.

Ballad of the Happy Christmas Wind

I am a happy Christmas wind;
I am courteous; I am kind.

I walked the way to Bethlehem town
Beside our Lady going down.

I know the inn she stood before;
I would have beaten down the door;

I thought on Mary and the Child;
I blew gently; I grew mild.

I ran ahead to find a house
To shelter Mary and her spouse.

I found a stable, loosed the door,
The cave they had been seeking for.

Because they had a place to bide
I was so glad, alone outside,

I ran across the hills for joy!
I waked a little shepherd boy,

And all the older shepherds stirred
At what they felt and what they heard

Of angel music, heavenly things!
I caught the song and gave it wings;

I ran across the midnight blue;
I ran across the ages, too;
I have it, have it here for you.

A Child is born for you again;
A Son is given, is given to men!
I am a singing wind. Amen.

A Nun Speaks to Mary

I

IN THE DAYS OF KING HEROD

You had no little maid, so I remember,
To help you sweep and tidy up the room,
To sit and watch with you that first December
Through shining twilights deep with golden gloom.

Through all those wistful days you had no mother
To know your wonder and to share your joy
Of fashioning—you could not let another!—
The darling swaddling garments for your Boy.

There was not any housewife to befriend you
The day word came to go to Bethlehem town;
No kinswoman bethought her to attend you
Of all the folk of David going down.

And when you held Him to your heart in wonder,
Emmanuel, God's Son, your Boy, the Word
Made flesh Who shook the skies with holy thunder,
In Bethlehem not any mother stirred.

II

SEQUEL

Now come again the sweet Isaian days,
Merciful, tender;
I know their loneliness; I dream their splendor.
Down their plain ways,
Mary, I come,
Confounded with this former shame, and dumb.
Take me in service, in complete surrender,
Waking and sleeping;
Take every daily task, take every duty,
Take little homely things as dusting, sweeping;
Change them into your heavenly housekeeping;
Touch them with Nazareth's most stricken beauty.
Think that my busy hands weave raiment fair
For Christ to wear;
Know that my hurrying feet
Run all your errands, Sweet;
And should they tarry,
Hear how I promise them,
My Lady Mary,
That they at length may go with you to Bethlehem.
And at the last let be
On those three mute and piteous, fearful days
When none of all earth's womenfolk is near you,
That you will have to help you and to cheer you
In little foolish ways
Poor, simple me;
That when you stand outside the inn, the night wind blowing,

I will be there
Adoring, knowing;
That if the whole wide world should have no room,
I will be waiting through whatever gloom
To be your resting place.—But this is heaven I dare!

So, let my promise be my prayer.
And do not seek for any cave at all
With patient kine and manger crib and stall
Beyond the gates of little Bethlehem town
To lay your dear Son down.
Mother, all fair,
Lay Him within my hungry arms to sleep;
Lay Him within my hungry heart to keep,
Adorable, holy,
Little and lowly.
And let earth's shepherds, let heaven's seraphim
So find me with you Christmas night, adoring, loving Him.

At Shadow Time

I watch the shadow folk creep down,
The white-faced stars climb up the sky;
I hear the little winds go by;
I see the far lights of the town.

I feel that peace is over them
And out of it this word I hear,
"The blessed time is very near,
The holy night at Bethlehem."

Over and over I repeat,
"O Bethlehem, O holy night,
O angel host, O starry light
Above a Baby small and sweet."

Then how I wish that I had been
A holy king, a shepherd dumb;
With what glad haste I would have come
To see the things that they have seen!

Scarce do I wish when lo! I see
A Lady in God's beauty dressed,
A sleeping Babe upon her breast,
Walk past me very quietly.

I think she comes a far, far way;
I think she walks the wide world's gloom,
Seeking somewhere a little room
In which her precious Child to lay.

But now her eyes grow large and bright;
I see that she has found a place,
And from the smile upon her face
The darkness blossoms into light.

"Here is a place, my little One,"
She whispers low, "where You may bide;
And room there is for me, beside;
A place of love it is, my Son.

"A place kept but for You alone;
And look You, what a beauteous thing,
Here You will reign, my little King,
Where love has built for You a throne."

Gently she lays her Babe to rest
In this place holy and apart;
The place I know; it is your heart
That loves this Child and loves Him best.

Then once again do I repeat,
"O Bethlehem, O holy night,
O angel host, O starry light
Above a Baby small and sweet."

I watch the shadows fall and hear
The little winds; I take your hand
In mine and we both understand
That Bethlehem is very near.

Wishes

The Christmas stars at Bethlehem
Shone very clear and bright;
Oh, may they shine with light divine
For you this Christmas night!

The Christmas winds at Bethlehem
Folded their wings away;
May every wind blow gently kind
For you on Christmas day.

The angel hosts at Bethlehem
Sang "Peace on earth to men;"
And may their song ring loud and long
Within your heart again.

The shepherds come to Bethlehem
Knelt in rapt wondering;
To Bethlehem, oh, haste with them
To see the little King!

The holy pair at Bethlehem
Looked upon them and smiled;
Would it might be your lot to see
These blest ones and the Child.

The little Babe at Bethlehem
Gave them His hand to kiss;
And oh, I pray your heart today
May know such joy as this.

Holy Communion
in a Hospital

All of my life I have come to You,
    walking erect, hands clasped,
    head a little bowed;
Finding my way to You through
    the Sunday, the every day crowd;
Kneeling to wait till You came to me
    in your own inexplicable way,
Leaving me shaken with love and
    with less than nothing to say;
Always I came to You so; always
    until today.

Today you will come to me here
    in this room half-lighted,
    curtains a little drawn.
Never before have You sought me so,
    brought me Yourself at dawn.
Now You are helplessly here more
    than I, to feed me, to comfort, to bless;
Infinite, patient to bear with me
    pain's relentless caress;
Clothing me with Yourself, in the
    vesture of helplessness.

Ballade for the Queen
of the World

It is not innocent organdy and lace;
It is not aureoles of lady-blue
That make illustrious haloes for your face
To crown the girl, the woman that is you.
Don any raiment of whatever hue;
Wear it with all the terrible grace you dare;
Make it an open secret. But the clue?
Who clothes you with the wonder that you wear?

Grant you a woman's everlasting grace;
Her mystery, once old, that now is new;
Grant in the world's wide, ever-changing place
Beauty that can be beautiful and true.
Queens have worn futile crowns in beauty's lieu.
Who set on you your shining crown of hair?
This regal thing only a King could do.
Who clothes you with the wonder that you wear?

You wore mortality a little space,
Lady of tears and laughter, myrrh and rue,
Where seven swords of sorrow left sharp trace,
Whence seven joys their flaming splendor drew.
Bright as the sun from head to shining shoe,
Your majesty is here, is everywhere,
Too near to see, too palpable to view!
Who clothes you with the wonder that you wear?

Envoi

Queen of the world, for servitude I sue,
Naming that name which is reply and prayer.
My hands in yours, I swear a Dieu, a Dieu
Who clothes you in the wonder that you wear.

Ballade on Eschatology

(For the Hero of the Habitually Relaxed Grasp)

Detachment is a virtue, teachers say.
Then let me practice it without regret.
What do I hold beyond this short today?
What cherish that I shall not soon forget?
These small things upon which my heart is set
Are matters for a heart's relinquishings.
One ultimate matter do I cleave to yet;
This, I shall not forget the four last things.

Remembrance, in a thief's unnoted way,
Filches from me with neither leave nor let
My thousand petty deities of clay.
Perhaps my eyes are still a little wet;
Perhaps my heart may still a little fret.
Detachment is the stuff of sunderings.
Time, so they tell me, is a brave asset.
And I shall not forget the four last things.

Your voice, your eyes,—or are they blue or gray?
The day we said good-bye, the day we met;
Hills we have walked, birds, flowers, our work, our play;—
Memory, how do you aid me and abet?
Time closes round me with impalpable net.
I'll not advert to clay or crowns or wings.
I have no thing to lose, all things to get,
For I shall not forget the four last things.

Envoi

Lord, though by mortal tyrannies beset,
Immortal freedom in my wild heart sings.
A pauper comes to pay a pauper's debt.
God, I shall not forget the four last things.

★
O
HOLY
WOOD
OF CRIB
AND ROOD
TODAY LET BE
Y
O
U
R
CHRISTMAS TREE